Malcolm Hedding

The Celebration of the FEAST of TABERNACLES

INTERNATIONAL CHRISTIAN EMBASSY JERUSALEM

The Celebration of the Feast of Tabernacles / Malcolm Hedding

ISBN0-9765297-4-2

Copyright©2004 by:
International Christian Embassy Jerusalem – USA, Inc.
PO Box 332974, Murfreesboro, TN 37133

The International Christian Embassy Jerusalem was founded in 1980 as an act of comfort and solidarity with Israel and the Jewish people in their claim to Jerusalem.

From our headquarters in Jerusalem and through our branches and representatives in over 80 nations, we seek to challenge the church to take up its scriptural responsibilities towards the Jewish people, to remind Israel of the wonderful promises made to her in the Bible, and to be a source of practical assistance to all the people of the land of Israel.

.

CONTENTS

Introduction

The Feast of Tabernacles is one of the three great pilgrim feasts of the Bible. The other two great feasts are Passover or *Pesach*, and Pentecost or *Shavuot*. In some sense, all three of them have to do with the kingdom of God.

It can be said that Passover is the door to the kingdom. In other words, you only get into this kingdom by the shedding of blood, and that is true.

Pentecost is the power of the kingdom because the Feast of Pentecost celebrates the giving of the Word of God, and the coming of the Spirit of God. When the people of God live in the power of His Word, overshadowed by the power of His Spirit, then that is the coming of the kingdom of God in power.

And last, the Feast of Tabernacles is supremely the celebration of the triumph of the kingdom. It celebrates God's care and God's love, and the final triumph of the kingdom of God.

So the three great pilgrim feasts teach us about the door to the kingdom of God, the power of the kingdom of God, and finally, the triumph of the kingdom of God.

Feast of Tabernacles

To begin our study of the Feast of Tabernacles, let us turn to Leviticus 23.

[33] Then the LORD spoke to Moses, saying,

[34] "Speak to the children of Israel, saying: 'The fifteenth day of this seventh month *shall be* the Feast of Tabernacles *for* seven days to the LORD.

[35] On the first day *there shall be* a holy convocation. You shall do no customary work *on it.*

[36] For seven days you shall offer an offering made by fire to the LORD. On the eighth day you shall have a holy convocation, and you shall offer an offering made by fire to the LORD. It *is* a sacred assembly, *and* you shall do no customary work *on it.*

[37] 'These *are* the feasts of the LORD which you shall proclaim *to be* holy convocations, to offer an offering made by fire to the LORD, a burnt offering and a grain offering, a sacrifice and drink offerings, everything on its day—

[38] besides the Sabbaths of the LORD, besides your gifts, besides all your vows, and besides all your freewill offerings which you give to the LORD.

[39] 'Also on the fifteenth day of the seventh month, when you have gathered in the fruit of the land, you shall keep the feast of the LORD *for* seven days; on the first day *there shall be* a sabbath-*rest,* and on the eighth day a sabbath-*rest.*

[40] And you shall take for yourselves on the first day the fruit of beautiful trees, branches of palm trees, the boughs of leafy trees, and willows of the brook; and you shall rejoice before the LORD your God for seven days.

[41] You shall keep it as a feast to the LORD for seven days in the year. *It shall be* a statute forever in your generations. You shall celebrate it in the seventh month.
[42] You shall dwell in booths for seven days. All who are native Israelites shall dwell in booths,
[43] that your generations may know that I made the children of Israel dwell in booths when I brought them out of the land of Egypt: I *am* the LORD your God.' "   *(Leviticus 23:33-43)*

Then we turn to the New Covenant scriptures, and we go to the Gospel according to John. Here we have the record of Jesus attending the Feast of Tabernacles in chapter 7.

[1] After these things Jesus walked in Galilee; for He did not want to walk in Judea, because the Jews sought to kill Him. [2] Now the Jews' Feast of Tabernacles was at hand.   *(John 7:1-2)*

[37] On the last day, that great *day* of the feast, Jesus stood and cried out, saying, "If anyone thirsts, let him come to Me and drink." [38] He who believes in Me, as the Scripture has said, out of his heart will flow rivers of living water." [39] But this He spoke concerning the Spirit, whom those believing in Him would receive; for the Holy Spirit was not yet *given,* because Jesus was not yet glorified. (John 7:37-39)

A Feast of Joy

This great festival, as commanded in the Word of God, ran for eight days and culminated in the conclusion of the reading of the Torah (the five books of Moses). It is a feast of joy, a time when the people of God are to rejoice greatly.

The scriptures command that the people of God are to be a joyful people. We read again about this feast in Deuteronomy.

> [13] "You shall observe the Feast of Tabernacles seven days, when you have gathered from your threshing floor and from your winepress."
> *(Deuteronomy 16:13)*

And then, look at verses 14 and 15.

> [14] "and you shall rejoice in your feast, you and your son and your daughter, your male servant and your female servant and the Levite, the stranger and the fatherless and the widow, who *are* within your gates.
> [15] Seven days you shall keep a sacred feast to the LORD your God in the place which the LORD chooses, because the LORD your God will bless you in all your produce and in all the work of your hands, so that you surely rejoice."

The Feast of Tabernacles is a time of great joy, and the people of God are commanded to rejoice in the keeping of it. The kingdom of God is a joyful kingdom. Sometimes, however, you have to wonder about God's people when they have anything but joy.

Romans 14:17 says the kingdom of God is not eating and drinking. It is not majoring on minors or nonessentials. The kingdom of God is righteousness, peace and joy in the Holy Spirit. If we claim to be a part of this kingdom, we should be a joyful people.

There should be something in your heart this day that just overflows with joy. This is the reminder that the Feast of Tabernacles certainly gives us.

A Feast of Reliance

The Feast of Tabernacles is more than a feast of joy, according to the scriptures. It also is a feast of reliance. It declares that we are totally dependent upon God. The Feast of Tabernacles is partly about the ingathering of the harvest. This is why when we read the story of the Feast of Tabernacles, ultimately, the harvest that was given to the children of Israel was acknowledged to be a gift from God. We are totally reliant upon Him. Therefore, as the harvest comes in, we rejoice that He has cared for us, He has looked after us, and He has provided for us.

It is a wonderful thing to be totally dependent upon God. This is something that has to do with your attitude more than your actions. There should be an attitude in each one of us today that certainly makes us totally dependent upon God.

We are reminded that Jesus said seek first the kingdom of God and all these things will be added to you. So, our hearts should be totally directed toward the King and toward His kingdom. We are to be totally reliant upon this God for everything.

A Feast of Surrender

So, it is the feast of reliance; therefore, it is a feast of surrender, and of course, it is a feast of triumph. Moreover, it certainly underlines the fact that the God we serve is able to do everything for us, because He cares for us. He knows our every heartbeat and need and constantly invites us to trust Him as we travel through life.

Celebrating in the Wilderness

Let us say a few words about the elements of this feast as found in its first celebration.

The Wilderness – A Place of Provision

First of all, the Feast was celebrated in the wilderness. God brought His people out of bondage like an eagle that cares for its young, and He says that He brought them out on His wings. He cared for them, He clothed them, He fed them and He protected them. This was the remarkable experience of the Israelites in the wilderness.

This is why quite likely it is called the feast of the kingdom - because the people of God were totally dependent upon the provision of God in a very harsh and unforgiving environment. Nevertheless, they found His remarkable provision to be there morning after morning. All this reminds us of the elegist who says, "Great is Your faithfulness...Your mercies are new every morning" (Lamentations 3:23).

The lesson is sure: in God's kingdom His care for His children is complete. Now, think about that. In God's kingdom, His care for His children is complete.

I do not know what problems you are facing today, or what difficulties you have to overcome, but it is my joy to tell you that God's care for you is complete. There is nothing outside of His care for you. There is nothing that you are experiencing that He will not be able to take hold of and solve in His own special way.

The Feast of Tabernacles reminds us that we are serving a wonderful God - a God who cares for us, provides for us, and knows everything about our troubles and difficulties. He is a loving God.

The desert experience was meant to teach Israel this lesson, that He is a God who provides. This was very important because the demonstration of His power in the desert and the demonstration of His character, which is even more important in the desert, were to be a learning experience for them that would enable them to move into the Promised Land.

A Place of Worship

The Feast of Tabernacles reminds us that the most important thing for the child of God is to understand the character of God. So often we are taken up with what God can give us - His power, His deliverance, His gifts - and we should be. The Bible says we should appropriate *everything* God has purchased for us through the death of His Son on the cross.

However, if we are going to walk successfully through this life, we have to have an appreciation of who God is. That is why worship is so important to the child of God. Worship in its original form means to describe the worth of God. It was first called "**worth**ship" and then shortened to worship.

When we worship God - and that is not just on a Sunday, or a Saturday, or a midweek meeting when we gather, but when we worship God - we think of His character. We think of who He is.

That is why the Feast of Tabernacles in the desert experience required that they live in booths or tabernacles with a flimsy roof made out of branches of trees. In every way they were exposed to the elements.

So, how would they live? How would they survive? How would they endure? The Bible says, because of their great God who loved them and would care for them. So, it is a lesson in understanding the character of God.

A Place to Learn the Character of God

You can never, ever put your trust in someone if you do not know who they are. You have to know who they are. And, so the Bible talks of the glory of God.

The glory of God is not a feeling, or a sensation or a cloud, necessarily. It can be one of these as a consequence, but that is not the essence of the glory of God. The glory of God is His character. What a wonderful thing to come into His presence and to remember the attributes of His character if you have a problem.

I have a big problem at present. I'm not going to burden you with the nature of it. It is a massive giant, and it has challenged me for over a year. Nevertheless I'm filled with joy, because my focus is not upon this problem.

My focus is upon the character of God. And when I look at His character and I begin to describe it and then ascribe glory to it, my problem diminishes. It becomes quite insignificant when I think of this God and all that He is.

13

Who is this God? He is a faithful God! He is a righteous God! This God is bigger than any problem in the world. He is holy. He is the central force in the universe. He made everything. He flung out the stars.

This God is omniscient. He knows everything. Nothing escapes Him. This God is omnipresent. He is everywhere. He is here this day; He is with us. He delights to dwell with us. He is omnipresent.

This God is omnipotent. He is ALL powerful. Do you know what the word "all" means? It means all. In other words, there is no problem on earth that *this* God cannot deal with. And when I lift my heart into His presence, that is worship. When I begin to talk to myself about His character, that is worship.

Worship is not only using your vocal cords in songs. Worship is when you talk to yourself about who He is. Suddenly, His presence fills your heart because you know who He is.

This was the lesson that the Israelites were supposed to have learned in the wilderness. That is why He led them in such a careful way before He took them to the Promised Land. He did not want to expose them to war and conflict because He knew that they were not ready for it.

The first lesson of discipleship that they needed was to understand who He is. If they could understand who He is, and see His faithfulness written on the sands of their experience in the desert, then He had no doubt that they would be emboldened to believe Him when they had to go to the Promised Land. Why? Because in the Promised Land, there were giants.

Can you imagine this story? These people have been told about the Promised Land for years. Where are we going? We're marching to the Promised Land, day after day.

"Moses," they said, "what is the Promised Land like?" And Moses would respond, "I tell you, it's incredible! The most beautiful land in the whole world."

So, they get to the border of the Promised Land and they have a conference and decide to send out spies. The spies go to the Promised Land and they come back with a story of woe. "It is a great place! Look at these fruits and vegetables that we've brought back with us! The only problem is that it is inhabited by giants."

The wilderness experience, the Tabernacles experience, was supposed to have taught them that God is bigger and more faithful than any problem. You need water? No problem. He will provide it. You need food? No problem. He will send quail. You need protection and love? No problem. He will send a pillar of cloud by day and a pillar of fire by night.

Whatever you need, this God can do it. They were supposed to have learned that lesson. The God who provided in the wilderness was able to provide in the land of promise, even if that provision meant ridding them of their enemies. They could not believe that.

How do you face your giants? Do you withdraw in a fit of depression, have a pity party and bewail the fact that, "God doesn't love me"? I know after 30 years of pastoring and shepherding the flock of God that these are normal responses of the people of God, even though He has provided everything for them in His Son.

If He gave Him for us, says Paul, how will He not freely give us all things with Him? So, what is your problem today? What is my problem today?

The Feast of Tabernacles with its flimsy booths is going to challenge you about your understanding of the faithfulness of God – and your ability to be totally dependent upon Him.

This feast has wonderful instruction for us because preeminently the Feast of Tabernacles teaches us not to limit God. It teaches us to understand who God is and make this the main goal of our lives as His children. If you have to learn anything in life, then please make sure you concentrate on the character of God. Understand who He is.

Learn Not to Limit God

If you can understand who God is, then you will not limit Him. He is always bigger than our problems. Therefore our focus must remain on Him. The interesting thing about this God of ours is this: that our Promised Land is always entered into by means of a battle.

God has promised you many wonderful things in Jesus. But you have to press in to all that God has for you. The New Covenant scriptures detail so much of what God wants to do for us in our lives.

But, sometimes we Christians think that if we just have fellowship with God, go to church, tithe and have our quiet time, these wonderful things will just rub off on us. How many of you have discovered that that is just not true? If this were true, we would learn nothing about God. As a consequence, nothing gets consolidated in your life.

The principle of the giant and the Promised Land is that God in Jesus gives us wonderful things, but we have to fight or overcome obstacles to get them. This is the only way to get important spiritual realities worked into our lives.

It is the only way for us to be strengthened by the presence and power of God, and the only way for us to learn the ways of God, and to have the image of Jesus entrenched in our lives. That is the Promised Land for you and for me. You will find a giant or two in your life and you have to press in against that giant. You have to believe that God can subdue that giant.

Strange as it may seem, the giant is doing you a favor, because he is enabling you to have some great spiritual blessing entrenched in your life. I have asked the Lord why I have to grapple with this giant that has now been challenging me for over a year.

The answer the Lord gave to me is the following: "I'm training your hands for war in a new way and unless you tackle this giant, you will not learn how to war. I want to prepare you for conflicts ahead and, if you know how to fight and overcome this giant, you will be ready for My greater purpose."

I know today that He is with me. I'm assured of His character, so I'm learning how to use a BIG sword. When you have gone through a battle like Caleb and Joshua did, and have subdued the giant, the land you subsequently acquire will never easily be taken from under your feet. It is yours, and that is the principle.

You have to press in to the Promised Land and if you do, then the giant actually becomes a blessing and not an obstacle. He is enabling you to have the kingdom of God entrenched in your life. So when Joshua and Caleb walked away from a few giant-slaying incidents, let me tell you, they were stronger than they were before.

The Feast of Tabernacles was supposed to have taught them that. That is why the tabernacle they were commanded to build was a booth made of flimsy material and covered with leafy branches. It was symbolic of our total dependence upon God. This reminds me of the words of Jesus in Luke 6:46 when He said, "Why do you call me Lord, Lord, but you do not do what I say?" Seek first the kingdom of God and all these things will be added to you.

Rejoicing over the Law

The final day, or the eighth day, of the Feast of Tabernacles marks the conclusion of the annual reading of the five books of Moses. If you go to Israel and celebrate the Feast of Tabernacles, then you will find on that great and final day of the Feast, that all through the city, there are groups of Jewish people spilling out into the streets from the synagogues. They are holding the Torah high and rejoicing in the streets with much dancing. It is a wonderful sight to behold.

The truth is, the law of God triumphs over evil. That is the truth. It triumphs over evil, it triumphs over the world, and it resides in our hearts. This is cause for great rejoicing!

The interesting thing about the Word of God is that Jesus died so that this precious moral law could be placed in our hearts – so that we would live it out as a principle, spontaneously and joyfully. As a consequence, we do not want to lie anymore, and when we make a mistake and sin and lie, something in us says, "You need to repent of that." You feel very awkward, don't you?

Have you ever had that experience when you have done something sinful? There is something in you that says, "Hey! You shouldn't have done that. You need to repent of that."

That is the principle of the law in your life, and that is why it is fascinating to note that the Bible says that the essence of the new covenant is God putting His moral law into your heart. Jeremiah 31 and Romans 8 are vital passages in fully appreciating the redemptive work of Jesus.

> 31 "Behold, the days are coming, says the LORD, when I will make a new covenant with the house of Israel and with the house of Judah -
> 32 not according to the covenant that I made with their fathers in the day *that* I took them by the hand to lead them out of the land of Egypt, My covenant which they broke, though I was a husband to them, says the LORD.
> 33 But this *is* the covenant that I will make with the house of Israel after those days, says the LORD: I will put My law in their minds, and write it on their hearts; and I will be their God, and they shall be My people.
> 34 No more shall every man teach his neighbor, and every man his brother, saying, 'Know the LORD,' for they all shall know Me, from the least of them to

the greatest of them, says the LORD. For I will forgive their iniquity, and their sin I will remember no more." *(Jeremiah 31:31-34)*

So, here he says there will be this inner teacher ruling over our hearts. I'm sure that John the Apostle got this from this passage, for in 1 John he says you do not have to have a teacher. In writing this he is not contradicting the Word of God. You need teachers in the body of Christ (Ephesians 4:11).

What he is saying is that in your personal walk with God, you do not have to have a pastor walking at your side every day telling you: "The Bible says that we should not lie, cheat, commit adultery, covet, get angry or dabble in the occult." You do not have to have that anymore because when the law comes into your heart, it becomes a natural instructor. This is the power of the new covenant.

When you walk every day with Jesus, no one needs to teach you anymore. You know what it means to know the Lord. It is wonderful, isn't it? And that law is personified in the Person of Jesus.

The essence of the new covenant, according to Jeremiah 31, is the principle of the law getting into human hearts because of the death, burial and resurrection of Jesus. We're talking here about the moral or majestic law, commonly known as the Ten Commandments - not the ritual law. Let us look at Romans 8.

[3] For what the law could not do in that it was weak through the flesh, God *did* by sending His own Son in the likeness of sinful flesh, on account of sin: He condemned sin in the flesh,

[4] that the righteous requirement of the law might be fulfilled in us who do not walk according to the flesh but according to the Spirit. *(Romans 8:3-4)*

In other words, we were totally unable to keep the law. There was nothing wrong with the moral law; the problem was us – our flesh, or carnal nature. So Jesus came that the righteous requirement of the law might be fulfilled in us.

Hallelujah! So, now I can rejoice! On the eighth day of the Feast I can spin around for joy! The Feast reminds me of this incredible truth. In the Bible, eight is the number of resurrection. The first day of the week, Sunday, is the eighth day. Only God's resurrection power in Messiah can transform our lives, give us joy and enable us to reflect the character of God.

Rivers of Living Water

The Feast of Tabernacles is special because we are commanded to rejoice. According to John's gospel, on the last and great day of the Feast, Jesus stood up and said, "If anyone is thirsty, let him come to Me and drink." He said this as He watched them draw water from the Pool of Siloam, using a very beautiful silver jug.

If you have been in Israel in the late winter, it rains. These are the former rains. The wonderful blessing about Israel is that from the end of March to the end of September you can have a barbecue every day because the sun will shine. You can plan all sorts of outdoor events without any type of concern about the weather. It will not rain. It might get a bit cloudy, but it will not rain. That is why the Bible speaks about the former and the latter rains. The latter rains come in September or October.

For all these months – half of the year - there is not a drop of rain anywhere. Hopefully, the former rains were so good that your cisterns, dams and lakes, like the Sea of Galilee, were full so that you could make it through the long, hot summer.

Then, at the end of the long, dry summer, at the Feast of Tabernacles, they would draw water, which was a precious commodity by that time of year, from the Pool of Siloam and pour it out before the Lord. By this ritual they were saying, "Our dependence is upon You and our life support system is in You, God. Not in our own ability; not even in this water. Though we have little of it and we need it, we will just pour it out before you because we love You."

Jesus stood and looked at that and then He said, "If any man thirsts" (if you want real life – the meaning of Tabernacles – if you want the kingdom), "let him come to me. For out of his belly shall be a never-ending stream of water" (I will give you something that will sustain you every day) (John 7:37). There will never be a long, dry summer. Isn't that wonderful?

There will never be a long, dry summer in your life if you're walking with Jesus as you ought to be. Now, that is a challenge to us. I wonder how many Christians live in that type of provision. How are you doing today? Are you in the long, dry summer?

The Feast of Tabernacles tells us that God loves you. Do not limit Him! Do not withdraw from Him because of the giant in your life. Let that giant thrust you forward toward Him. Press in! Press in! Appropriate! It will lead to a new level of maturity.

I'm telling you that out of your life will flow a waterfall that will sustain you and from which, most important of all, others can drink.

Celebrating the Kingdom of God

The Feast of Tabernacles then declares God's triumph over all that is evil, both now and in the future. It is present-focusing and forward-looking.

The kingdom of God is a wonderful thing. We could spend hours talking about the kingdom of God, because the kingdom of God is not one thing only. For many people, the coming of the kingdom of God is all in the future, and that is true. It will arrive in a more visible, dramatic manifestation in the future. This is true.

But, the kingdom of God is also present now. When the Pharisees asked Jesus about the coming of the kingdom of God, He told them that the kingdom of God does not come with signs to be observed only but that the kingdom of God is in you and therefore around you (Luke 17:20-21). (The Greek indicates that the kingdom will be "in you" but as a consequence "in your midst.")

He said that the kingdom of God is "in you" and therefore it is "around you," as if what is in you is constantly overflowing. We have to ask ourselves if the kingdom of God is so entrenched in our lives that it is overflowing to people around us?

Just imagine what will happen when the church gets this message of Tabernacles. Just imagine! Sometimes I think that we live at a spiritual level that is way below God's plan and desire for us.

God has a Promised Land, and the only thing that keeps us from entering it is our problem: the giant. "I can't do this. I can't speak. Me? No! Never! I'm useless." Well, I have news for you: you *are* useless! So get over it!

You see, God can make you speak and He can be your ability. I have a personal testimony about that. I was a born stutterer – could not speak two words without stuttering. I was taken out of school to get speech therapy and spent my school years feeling humiliated by my inability to communicate.

The speech therapist would come into the class and ask for Malcolm Hedding, and I would have to get up and walk out of class because I was the little boy that couldn't speak.

Then Jesus met me when I was 14. I won't tell you the story, but it was amazing. I met Him in the garden of my home where I opened the Bible, and read this: "Also the heart of the rash will understand knowledge and the tongue of the stammerer will be ready to speak clearly" (Isaiah 32:4).

I did not know much of the Bible then. I had no idea whether Genesis was in the New Testament or in the Old Testament, and yet, I opened the Bible on the only verse that speaks of stuttering.

Jesus said to me, "Now, I'm going to come to your life. I'll take this giant away and you'll speak for Me." So, whatever your problem is, get over it. Your power is not in yourself.

26

Trust God! Get out of the boat! You'll find you can walk on water. Face your giant. Do not limit God! That is the message of Tabernacles for Israel and for us – the message that we glean from the wilderness experience.

God says, "What is your problem? So, there are giants there? I knew that! Who fed you? Who clothed you? Who provided for you? You think I cannot slay a giant?"

God's Care for All People

All of Israel was instructed to gather four species. They were to take four types of leafy branches and put them together. These four species were willow, palm, etrog and myrtle. These are said to represent the four types of people in all the world. What are the four types of people in all the world?

• First, those who bear righteous fruit but have no righteous fragrance. In other words, they do things, they are task-oriented, but they are difficult to get along with.

• Then there are those who bear fruit, who do things AND have a sweet fragrance about their lives. That is the way it should be. Let us do things, but in a way that we bless people.

• Thirdly, there are those who have a sweet fragrance, but no fruit. In other words, they are very sweet, and lovely, but you can never get them to do anything.

• And then, there are those who have neither fruit nor fragrance. People who have just never been touched by the grace of God.

What does this tell us? It tells us that God cares for all types of people, because at the Feast of Tabernacles the four species would then be waved to the four corners of the earth, thus demonstrating God's care and love for all peoples.

His message and kingdom begins with Israel, but impacts the whole world. The Feast of Tabernacles, through the symbolism of the four species, acknowledges this. When the Jewish people hold the four species up and wave them to the four corners of the earth, they demonstrate that God has a peculiar care for every human being.

That is quite an important principle, because it tells me that our outreach to people, as the church of God, should be couched in love and care. That is a challenge. There should be something in our projection of ministry that tells people, "You know, we care for you...it is not about getting you into church to swell the numbers, or getting you to join our group so that it is bigger and better."

The Feast of Tabernacles reminds us that people are important and our outreach should be punctuated with a sense of care. When people feel cared for, they feel loved and they feel drawn to the message.

So it was that the four species represented the plan of God to use Israel as a mechanism to reach the world. The focus is not just on Israel, it is upon the world. This, as we've seen, is certainly the very reason why God called Israel into existence through the great patriarch Abraham when God said to him, "In you all the families of the earth will be blessed." Israel, you are not an end in yourself. No, you are a means to an end!

This is ultimately about the nations. You (Israel) are a *means* to an end. The Feast of Tabernacles reminds us of that. That is why Zechariah 14 tells us that ultimately all the nations should celebrate the Feast of Tabernacles, and will, in the reign of Messiah.

> [16] And it shall come to pass *that* everyone who is left of all the nations which came against Jerusalem shall go up from year to year to worship the King, the LORD of hosts, and to keep the Feast of Tabernacles.
> [17] And it shall be *that* whichever of the families of the earth do not come up to Jerusalem to worship the King, the LORD of hosts, on them there will be no rain.
> [18] If the family of Egypt will not come up and enter in, they *shall have* no *rain;* they shall receive the plague with which the LORD strikes the nations who do not come up to keep the Feast of Tabernacles.
> *(Zechariah 14:16-18)*

Now, this will happen in the messianic age. So, there again the imagery (or the lessons of the Feast of Tabernacles) is consistent with all the other passages of the Word of God – even with Jesus. Nations refusing to celebrate the Feast in the age to come will have no rain. It's all about our support system and a limitless God who can do anything. It means coming to Him and having your life drenched with His love and water so that every day means drinking from a well that never runs dry.

Israel's Central Role

The Feast of Tabernacles reminds us that Israel is the mechanism that will bring in the final manifestation of the kingdom of God. There is coming a day when the Messiah will reign from Jerusalem. Israel is the platform that brings that into reality.

In Acts 1, the disciples were about to launch out on their worldwide mission. Jesus had commissioned them to go to every nation and to speak to every creature.

They were gathered on the Mount of Olives for a final meeting. They were now going to take leave of Him and He was going to return to the right hand of glory. Nevertheless they had this burning question in their minds, and they were determined to get it in before He left. "Lord, will you at this time restore the kingdom to Israel?" (Acts 1:6). That is, will you now raise up David's throne?

Is this the time of the morning star? When the night is swept away and the dawn breaks over humanity in the form of a throne that is like a star in its glory, upon which the Messiah will sit? "Is this, Lord," they were asking, "the time that you're going to do that?" In other words, what is your program? What is your agenda?

> [7] And He said to them, "It is not for you to know times or seasons which the Father has put in His own authority.
> [8] But you shall receive power when the Holy Spirit has come upon you; and you shall be witnesses to Me in Jerusalem, and in all Judea and Samaria, and to the end of the earth." *(Acts 1:7-8)*

Jesus does not deny that this kingdom is coming. He just says it is not the time because, before this time comes, they, the disciples, have to go into all the world. The Father most certainly knows the time of His Son's coming and He will bring it about at the end of the age.

The restoration of Israel in our time is a herald of this coming dispensation, if you will, of the Feast of Tabernacles. It is the preparation for this great day when the Son of David will set up His throne and rule over the nations with a rod of iron.

This is why Israel is so important, and the reason why we stand with her and pray for her. This is why we comfort her and bless her and come alongside her. We understand the purpose of God and we are like the people of Issachar who understand the times and know what God is doing in Israel (1 Chronicles 12:32).

The kingdom is coming! The great period of Tabernacles, of triumph; the great period of joy is about to break in upon the world. This, I believe, should infuse every one of us with a great sense of expectation, excitement and joy and it should make us more than ever dependent upon this great God. Now, more than ever, dedicate your life to Him and make sure that He is everything to you.

The Annual Celebration of the International Christian Embassy Jerusalem

No discussion about the Feast of Tabernacles would be complete without talking about the Celebration of the Feast that the International Christian Embassy Jerusalem began in 1980. Since that time, literally tens of thousands of Christians from all over the world have come up during the Feast of Tabernacles to rejoice before their Messiah King in Jerusalem…and to express their love and gratitude to the Jewish people for all that they have received through them.

They are the vehicle of world redemption. They are the custodians of the Word of God; they are the mediators of the great covenants. Paul says, we share in their spiritual things, therefore we are indebted to them (Romans 15:27).

This phenomenon of thousands of Christians coming up to Jerusalem has been and is a prophetic statement from the God of Heaven. The fact that this has happened and is happening is a miracle.

Even in the worst years of conflict in Israel, such as the Intifada, we continued to draw thousands of Christians to Zion. Where they come from, I do not know. I can only believe that there is something so important about this event that the God of Israel is putting it in the hearts of men and women and saying to them, this year you will have to go to Jerusalem.

The stories we hear are phenomenal. A little 7-year-old girl from the United States, for instance, came to her mother last year and said, "God has told me to dance in Jerusalem." Well, one thing led to the next, and she had this burning desire to worship in Jerusalem. So her mother brought her to the Feast of Tabernacles.

The most amazing thing is that when we put our post-Feast magazine together, we picked a photograph for the front cover that was of this little girl with her arms uplifted, her little face toward heaven, worshipping God in Zion. When her mother received the magazine in the mail, it was a type of unbelievable confirmation. This child's little face went all over the world in our magazine, and we had no idea of the unique story behind this picture.

Only the God of the Bible could have done this! Why? Because it constitutes a prophetic statement. He called this gathering into being, and He alone has brought the participants year by year to Zion.

It is a declaration of the soon-coming purpose of God. It is a type of sign to the world that the final manifestation of the kingdom of God is about to break in upon the world through the nation of Israel. This coming kingdom will usher in the dispensation of the times of the Feast of Tabernacles.

It is true to say that redemptive history has three segments. We have a Passover segment from Moses to Jesus. We have a Pentecost segment in which we are now living. That is the time of the Spirit of God and the gathering in of a harvest from every nation and corner of the world.

However, we are moving to the final great segment of human history, which will be the Tabernacles segment. God has raised up this prophetic sign with participants from all over the world as a herald of His soon-coming purpose. I can only believe that. It is a herald that the kingdom of God is about to triumph.

Messiah's feet will shortly stand on the Mount of Olives and when they do, His visible kingdom will break in on the world and He will rule the nations with a rod of iron. They will neither destroy nor hurt in His holy mountain; they will not learn war anymore and the knowledge of the Lord will cover the earth as the waters cover the sea. This will be the age of Tabernacles and, my friends, it will be an age of unparalleled joy.

We have the kingdom now, in our hearts. However, we also look forward to this amazing time. The Bible describes it like this in the book of Revelation.

³ And I heard a loud voice from heaven saying, "Behold, the tabernacle of God *is* with men, and He will dwell with them, and they shall be His people. God Himself will be with them *and be* their God."
(Revelation 21:3)

This is the essence of the Feast of Tabernacles: whether it be in the wilderness, or radiating from a throne over all the earth, it means that the Tabernacle of God will forever be with men.

⁴ "And God will wipe away every tear from their eyes; there shall be no more death, nor sorrow, nor

crying. There shall be no more pain, for the former things have passed away."

[5] Then He who sat on the throne said, "Behold, I make all things new." And He said to me, "Write, for these words are true and faithful."

(Revelation 21:4-5)

We have a marvelous destiny, and this should excite us.

Lastly, this tremendous phenomenon of the Feast of Tabernacles celebration sponsored by the International Christian Embassy Jerusalem is also a warning. Israel's journey has been a long and a suffering one. She has birthed the written Word, the Bible, and the Living Word, the Messiah, for the world.

Because of this, she has been the target of the devil, who has consistently sought to liquidate her so that the redemptive plan of God can be frustrated. Now, she has gone home for the last time, to bring in the kingdom of God for the whole world.

Therefore, this final return of Israel will be challenged by the powers of darkness in a way that the world has never seen. This means, dear friends, that our celebration of the Feast of Tabernacles in Jerusalem is a warning to the world, a statement that in this people remains the purpose of God.

The church has not replaced Israel. She (Israel) retains a national destiny. She, too, like all peoples of the earth, must be saved through the once-for-all finished work of the Messiah on the cross. However, she does have a national destiny, and that destiny is to birth the redemptive plan of God for the world. She has gone back to bring the King of the kingdom to this world.

The Bible does say we have to be careful what we do with the Jewish people because they are the apple of His eye. She is the pregnant woman of Revelation 12, and we have to be careful how we handle a pregnant woman.

So, to conclude, the final day of triumph will come. This is what the Feast of Tabernacles is all about. That is, the glorious age of Tabernacles will be ushered in, but God is calling upon us to be a people of prayer and intercession.

Israel needs our prayers as does the world. Remember, the purpose of God is not just Israel, it is the nations. But, we need to be a people who are praying for Israel. This great conflict that will erupt and is erupting will only be solved by men and women of prayer; i.e., people who look beyond the complexities of the region, people who are prepared to look beyond the giant in the region.

People have said to me time and time again, they have no idea what the solution is to the Middle East conflict. In the natural, that is absolutely true. And if you look at the conflict with your natural eyes, you will get depressed and the problems will loom greater than the solutions.

However, if you remember the message of the Feast of Tabernacles, that we have a wonderful God, a limitless God, a God who can be trusted, then you know that He, in the end, will solve this problem in a way that He alone will get the glory. In addition, the nations will know that He is God. I have a sneaking suspicion that He is allowing this conflict to get more complicated with every passing day so that through this, He will demonstrate to the world who He is.

I close with Ezekiel 39. Listen to these words:

[7] "So I will make My holy name known in the midst of My people Israel, and I will not *let them* profane My holy name anymore. Then the nations shall know that *I am* the LORD, the Holy One in Israel.
[8] Surely it is coming, and it shall be done," says the Lord GOD. "This *is* the day of which I have spoken." *(Ezekiel 39:7-8)*

My dear friends, the Feast of Tabernacles puts our eyes upon a God who cannot be limited.

It is the joy of the International Christian Embassy Jerusalem to celebrate this event year by year so that we can lift Him up, declare His character, and trust Him fully.

Your Embassy in Jerusalem

The International Christian Embassy Jerusalem was founded in 1980 as an act of solidarity with the Jewish people in recognition of their 3000-year-old claim and connection to Jerusalem. Today, the ICEJ stands at the forefront of a growing mainstream movement of Christians worldwide who share a love and concern for Israel and an understanding of the biblical significance of the modern ingathering of the Jews to the land of their forefathers.

The Embassy's work and witness is founded on the mandate of Isaiah 40:1, "Comfort, comfort my people..." From our headquarters in Jerusalem and through our branches and representatives in over 80 nations, we seek to challenge the Church to take up its scriptural responsibilities towards the Jewish people, to remind Israel of the wonderful promises made to her in the Bible and to be a source of practical assistance to all the people of the land of Israel.

Supporting Israel

AID PROJECTS: For 30 years the ICEJ has been building relationships, fostering reconciliation and sharing God's love in Israel through a wide variety of humanitarian projects that respond to many areas of pressing social need. From providing emergency relief to victims of terror to caring for elderly Holocaust survivors in their homes, ICEJ AID projects have touched almost every community and people group in the land.

ADVOCACY: Through our network of international representatives, we raise up support for the people of Israel through solidarity rallies, teaching events, and advocacy campaigns. We engage with pastors, governments and local Jewish communities, recognizing our scriptural responsibility to stand with the Jewish people, while promoting Christian tourism and understanding of Israel.

ALIYAH: In the 1980s the ICEJ was at the forefront of global efforts to support the persecuted Soviet Jews. Since then we have helped 100,000 return 'home' to Israel and offered practical support to assist thousands more upon arrival in the land. ICEJ aliyah efforts continue in the former Soviet republics, with new initiatives in Europe and North America, and among the next generation of Jewish youth.

Proclaiming Justice

ANTI-SEMITISM: The ICEJ is called to confront the rising tide of hostility that threatens the nation of Israel and Jewish community worldwide. The ICEJ's historic partnership with Israel's Yad Vashem Holocaust Remembrance Center seeks to mobilize Christians to confront anti-Semitism in all its forms. In addition, the ICEJ is engaged in ongoing efforts to provide accurate daily news reports from Israel, church-wide educational efforts and hard-hitting advocacy campaigns.

PERSECUTION: Islamic extremism is not just a threat to Israel, but is responsible for the persecution of Christians and oppression of women throughout the Middle East. So, in addition to efforts to assist our beleaguered brethren in the Palestinian areas, we offer support to hundreds of African refugees who have fled Muslim warlords in Sudan and persecution in Egypt. ICEJ Operation Hope is now helping hundreds of these destitute Christians find hope and safety in Israel.

Teaching Truth

AT THE FEAST: The ICEJ is probably best known for hosting the Christian celebration of the Feast of Tabernacles - a multicultural event that draws thousands of pilgrims to Jerusalem from 70 nations for teaching, worship and prayer. As the largest annual tourist event in Israel, the Feast has a tremendous economic and spiritual impact on ordinary Israelis, and points to the day when all the earth will worship the One true God in Zion.

TO THE NATIONS: Reaching out in many languages through radio, print and electronic media, the ICEJ educates Christians all over the world about Israel's unique calling, political situation and social challenges. Embassy speakers undertake international teaching tours that have brought the prophetic message of Israel's restoration to churches in Europe, the Americas, Africa, India, Asia and beyond.

ACROSS GENERATIONS: Grafted, the ICEJ Young Adults program, seeks to raise up a new generation of Christian leaders who will grasp God's covenant purposes for the nation of Israel. Teams minister to youth groups and churches abroad and host short-term Grafted tours in Israel offering a unique blend of study and service opportunities for young adults aged 18-30.

ICEJ BIBLICAL ZIONISM SERIES

The Basis of Christian Support for Israel

The basis of Christian support for Israel is found in God's promises to Abraham. The Abrahamic covenant declared God's love for the world and his establishment of a people through which to redeem the world. Israel's unique calling is still in force today and her return home to the land given to Abraham is evidence of that. ISBN# 0-9765297-0-X

The Heart of Biblical Zionism

Clear biblical principles concerning God's dealings with Israel and the nations are the framework for an accurate interpretation of God's promises and calling on national Israel. Biblical Zionism is clearly defined and put in the correct theological context in this teaching.
ISBN# 0-9765297-1-8

The Great Covenants of the Bible

This exciting study of the four great covenants of the Bible also refutes Replacement Theology which teaches that the church has replaced Israel and Israel no longer has a unique call or destiny.
ISBN# 0-9765297-2-6

The New Testament and Israel

The New Testament validates a number of Old Testament doctrines concerning Israel. Foremost it affirms that God has not gone back on His promises to Israel.
ISBN# 0-9765297-3-4

The Celebration of the Feast of Tabernacles

The Feast of Tabernacles is a celebration of the triumph of the kingdom of God and as such is now celebrated annually by Christians around the world.
ISBN# 0-9765297-4-2

THIS TEACHING SERIES IS ALSO AVAILABLE IN CD AND DVD FORMAT

To schedule Rev. Hedding to speak, or to request further information about this series or the ICEJ contact us Call: (615) 895-9830 or go to: www.icejusa.org

Word From Jerusalem

Sign up to receive our free flagship monthly magazine featuring articles about ICEJ aid projects, special events and advocacy campaigns in Israel and across the globe.

In-depth, and timely Bible teaching, news commentary and special reports offer unparalleled insight into modern-day Israel's unique call, her struggle, her achivements and history.

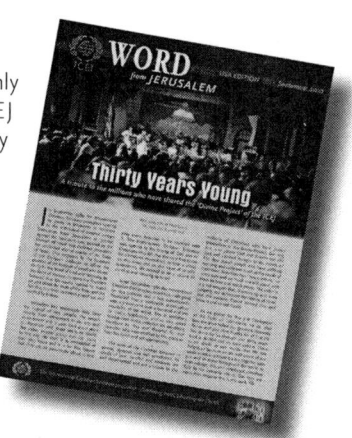

SIGN UP TODAY AT: WWW.ICEJUSA.ORG/WFJ
or by calling (615) 895-9830

INTERNATIONAL
CHRISTIAN
EMBASSY
JERUSALEM

P.O. Box 332974 • Murfreesboro, TN 37133 • www.icejusa.org